~~I BEGIN~~
AGAIN?

*Answers to the
Deepest Questions of Life*

RICHARD BEWES

BARBOUR
PUBLISHING, INC.
Uhrichsville, Ohio

CONTENTS

QUESTIONS

Does God care about our world?

What can I do about my messed-up life?

Does the Christian faith offer anything that can help me?

How often I have heard these questions! As the pastor of a large London church, I meet many people who are searching, people who want a reason for living, companionship along the way, hope for the future.

I have written this book for searching people. At the very beginning I want to state my firm convictions:

Yes, God cares—not only about the world, but about you and me personally.

Any life, however messed up, can be put back together again.

The Christian faith offers more hope and happiness than most of us dream of.

Join me in taking a quick look at what

Christians believe. As you read, I hope another question will be forming in your mind—perhaps the most important question you will ever ask:

How can I become a Christian?

IN THE BEGINNING

It is highly unlikely that our complex world was created by mere chance. Still, we cannot automatically conclude that a loving God created it and takes a personal interest in us. First we must address some genuine questions. For example, doesn't science conflict with religion?

Many people think so, but such a conflict is unnecessary.

It is quite certain that most scientific textbooks now in use will be superseded and unread within just a few years. It is equally certain that the first book of the Bible, the Book of Genesis, will continue to be published and read throughout the rest of history.

This is because science and the Bible have very different roles. To suggest that they cover the same ground is absurd. It would be the same as suggesting that the ear can taste, or the eye can smell.

The role of science is to probe the observable world, while the role of the Bible is to reveal the unobservable. Science, in its ongoing task of observing the world, must answer the question, How? How did it all come about? What processes were at work?

But the Bible does not focus on that question. Rather, it answers the question that science can never begin to answer: Why? Why are we here? What is the purpose of it all, the basic reason for our being alive?

In these age-old documents we find luminous answers to our questions. Rather than analyzing how precisely the creation came about, Genesis offers a timeless account that has spanned every century and continues to captivate us with its rhythmic, majestic cadences. Genesis tells us that God is a God of order and that everything happens stage by stage, according to His plans.

But if we look to Genesis to learn exactly how the various stages were achieved, we are asking the wrong questions. God inspired the author of Genesis to write, not as a scientist (that would be too narrow), nor as a news reporter (that would be too easily forgotten), but in terms that the world will always remember regardless of the century of culture.

Here in the Bible is a God-centered declaration about this world that is our home. It can speak with equal power to South Americans and Africans; to jazz musicians, computer programmers, and factory workers; to children and professors, to diplomats and laborers, to prisoners and presidents.

THE GUIDEBOOK

Voltaire, a stern critic of eighteenth-century Christianity, predicted that within a century the Bible would be obsolete. Today, more than two hundred years after Voltaire's death, it is the world's best-selling book.

Why has the Bible lasted so long and had such enormous influence? Where did it come from?

The Bible claims to present God's words. Repeatedly the Old Testament prophets say, "Thus says the Lord." New Testament writers also claim to speak for God. Paul the Apostle says, "We speak, not in words taught us by human wisdom but in words taught by the Spirit" (1 Corinthians 2:13).

"You must understand that no prophecy of Scripture came about by the prophet's own interpretation. For prophecy never had its origin in the will of man, but men spoke from God as they were carried along by the Holy Spirit" (2 Peter 1:20–21).

Jesus' own attitude toward the Old

Testament carries much weight. "The Scripture," He said, "cannot be broken" (John 10:35). "It is easier for heaven and earth to disappear than for the least stroke of a pen to drop out of the Law" (Luke 16:17). Jesus criticized the religious leaders of His time for their attitude. He told them, "You nullify the word of God by your tradition that you have handed down" (Mark 7:13).

Too many people criticize the Bible or dismiss it as irrelevant when in reality they have never thoughtfully examined it. To the inquirer who demands, "Prove to me that the Bible is true and relevant for today," I reply, "No, you prove it."

Get hold of the Gospel of Luke and start there. Or take a piece of literature that has been more widely distributed around the world than any other fragment—the Gospel of John. Philosophers and theologians have pored over it, written reams about it, dissected and analyzed it—and what is it, after all, but a pamphlet written many years ago by a man trained in commercial fishing!

Plato, Augustine, and Josephus are read only by specialists today. Even poor Voltaire is rarely read outside the classroom. Voltaire's prophecy never came true. In fact, within a hundred years of his death, his house was turned into a Bible warehouse.

By contrast, the booklets written by such common people as Matthew the tax collector and John the fisherman have taken—and continue to take—hundreds of millions of readers by storm.

JUST A PIECE OF MEAT?

At times we may be half persuaded that we are little more than collections of biochemical reactions trapped in an impersonal universe in which the words love, beauty, and purpose have no meaning.

I am just a piece of meat.

RAQUEL WELCH

But every now and then something happens. . .and the suspicion creeps into our minds that we are much more significant than mere machines.

Several years ago, the world watched the televised drama of a dramatic rescue on the Potomac River near Washington, D.C., following the crash of a jet airliner into the water. Rescue launches and helicopters were everywhere. Suddenly a bystander hurled himself into the water and started swimming toward a drowning girl. Heedless of the media, the police, and the rescue workers, he reached the girl and pulled her to safety.

Was this event entirely predictable? Was Lenny Skutnik not really responsible for his actions—were they all programmed by his genetic inheritance or environmental influences?

Many of today's thinkers believe that we are products of external forces beyond our control. But such theories rarely hold much appeal in a moment of crisis. A heroic act, a sacrificial endeavor, can explode these theories and reduce them to mere intellectual exercises.

Most of us, deep down, know we are able to love, to innovate, to choose, and to worship. We know we are persons, not machines or hunks of meat. A thousand incidents like the one involving Lenny Skutnik remind us that we have, at the core of our being, something that machines and animals do not possess—a moral and spiritual dimension.

We can say *I love*, and *I should*, and *I will*.

THE GREAT DEFECTION

At the end of a five-thousand-mile air flight, nonstop, I marveled at the technological feat that had just been accomplished. *How far humankind has progressed,* I mused as I stepped out of the airliner.

Abruptly my thoughts changed. All around were soldiers intently clutching AK-47 machine guns. This was no smiling welcome. Mistrust and suspicion were on every face.

In fact, men and women have not progressed morally or spiritually after all these centuries. Our technology may be advanced, but we use it to harm ourselves and one another. The world overflows with fear, hatred, murder, and destruction. Where do these things come from?

The world, as originally created, was good. Then rebellion and evil intruded. Did they come from another universe? An alternative system? No. The Bible has no place for "dualism"—the idea that evil and good are equally strong. The only original and eternal phenomenon is God and His goodness. Evil was an interruption.

God created the human race and put it in a good world. He did this because He loves us. He left us free to return His love by serving Him and helping each other. But love can never be enforced, or it ceases to be love.

When God made us free, He made us entirely free—free to love, free also to rebel. We might wish we had not been given this moral capacity to choose God's way or our own. But if we were not free to choose, what would we be like? We would be programmed, like machines. We would not be made in God's image. We would be unable to love.

The first chapters of the Bible may describe creation, but they also go on to speak of a terrible misuse of freedom. Human beings freely chose to disobey. They chose to deviate from God's plan, to rebel against His loving authority. When they did this, they cut themselves off from God's goodness. They separated themselves from His life-giving power.

In choosing evil, they chose death. And the results of their choice are still plaguing us today.

The great problem of the human race is that, unless God intervenes, we are cut off from the creator. It is not that we await a future assessment of our deeds, a weighing up of good deeds against bad, with the final verdict trembling in the balance. The sentence has already been passed. The Bible is clear: "The soul who sins is the one who will die" (Ezekiel 18:20). "The wages of sin is death" (Romans 6:23).

We may hope that by performing decent and generous acts we might tip the scales in our favor. But in the end it makes no difference—the mass of evil is too great. "There is no difference, for all have sinned and fall short of the glory of God" (Romans 3:22–23).

We may feel that by affirming Christian beliefs and trusting in such church ceremonies as baptism or confirmation, we may enter God's friendship. But these events are helpful only if they lead us to a personal relationship with Jesus Christ. Without this reality, our moral efforts or religious observances count for nothing.

The Bible's stark diagnosis of our condition is shocking. But it is as well for us to realize that if we try to manage through life and eternity by our own moral efforts, we are bound to fail. It can't be done. If it could, Jesus would not have needed to come to earth and die on the cross for us.

It is to Jesus Christ that we must now turn.

THE GOODNESS
OF JESUS

In his novel *The Plague*, in which a city is stricken by a raging epidemic, Albert Camus offers the reader a grim choice. You can identify with the doctor, who fights the plague but thereby fights against God's will, or you can identify with the priest, who deliberately refuses to combat the scourge and thus increases his community's toll of misery and death.

Which will you choose? Or are those the only choices? Christianity would respond with a resounding "No." The Bible introduces us to Jesus. Born two thousand years ago in a Middle Eastern occupied country, He did God's will perfectly. He also worked tirelessly to relieve human suffering.

Jesus consistently took the side of the outcast, the poor, and the handicapped. He wept at the tomb of his friend Lazarus (John 11:35), challenging the powers of death and despair and throwing them back.

Jesus cared for His struggling, alienated world. He loved it and dedicated Himself in self-sacrifice on its behalf. He died for it outside the city in the place reserved for criminals, rejected by all but a very few of those closest to Him.

Who was this person who went knowingly, willingly to die for the sins of the world?

His disciples, the twelve men who ate, traveled, and ministered with Him, clashed on many issues, but about Jesus they were of one mind: No one could pin anything sordid or unworthy on Him.

" 'He committed no sin, and no deceit was found in his mouth.' When they hurled their insults at him, he did not retaliate; when he suffered, he made no threats" (1 Peter 2:22–23).

Remarkably, Jesus Himself claimed to be sinless (see John 7:18, 8:46). This is uncharacteristic of holy people. Ordinarily, the closer people get to God, the more worthless they feel. Not so Jesus. He hated self-righteousness and conceit, yet He said of His relationship to God the Father, "I always do what pleases him" (John 8:29).

Jesus' goodness is very attractive. In fiction goodness sometimes seems sickly, and evil fascinating. Real life turns the tables: Evil makes the world gray, a monotonous wasteland of despair, but goodness creates a profusion of loving relationships and inspiring possibilities.

Across the ages, Jesus' shining goodness has inspired and attracted His millions of followers, who are willing to die for Him if necessary.

JESUS: GOD WITH US

Jesus' disciples, men who were exposed to His teaching and His goodness, were not afraid to tell the world they believed He was much more than a good man. The disciples believed Jesus was God.

The disciples saw Jesus, in the face of the strict Jewish monotheism of that time, accept the worship of others.

He did this after a storm on Lake Galilee. The disciples, caught in the high winds, panicked. Jesus walked across the water to them and climbed into their boat, and the wind died down. The people in the boat worshiped Him, and Jesus did not object.

"My Lord and my God!" (John 20:28) exclaimed the formerly doubting disciple, Thomas, on meeting with Jesus after His resurrection. Again, Jesus did not discourage such belief.

The disciples saw Jesus forgive the sins of others.

A man might be able to forgive someone

who has injured him, but how could he intervene in someone else's quarrel and forgive the guilty person? No wonder Jesus' critics exclaimed, "He's blaspheming! Who can forgive sins but God alone?" (Mark 2:7).

The disciples heard Jesus make claims that could be true only if He is God.

John recorded some of these claims in chapters five to eight of his Gospel. For example, in chapter eight Jesus uses God's name, *I am,* for Himself, so provoking an attack with stones from the infuriated Jewish listeners.

John's Gospel portrays a man who claims to be the world's Savior and Messiah, the judge of all mankind and the center of all truth. He is not simply one light among many in the history of world luminaries; He is the original source light from which all other lights can only borrow.

The disciples knew Jesus well, and they concluded that He is God. We have to look at their evidence and make up our minds.

It is not the slightest use saying that Jesus was simply a great teacher. If He was wrong about His relationship to the eternal Father, then He was far worse than mistaken. He was either a lying imposter or a deluded megalomaniac.

Just occasionally we run across people who opt for one of these two choices—but they tend to have some strange kink or unusual grudge. Most people are ready to affirm Jesus' essential goodness and sanity.

So one option remains: If Jesus was indeed good and trustworthy, then He spoke the truth about Himself. Here is God Himself, "Immanuel" (Matthew 1:23), "God with us."

Can we believe this? Will we believe this? Our reaction will determine the course of the rest of our lives.

THE DEATH OF JESUS

It is not possible to talk seriously about Jesus Christ without looking at His death. His execution upon a Roman cross was at the center of His mission of love to our world. "The Son of Man," He said, "did not come to be served, but to serve, and to give his life as a ransom for many" (Matthew 20:28).

Jesus without the cross is like William the Conqueror without a sword or Shakespeare without a pen. God came to us in Jesus Christ for the specific purpose of dying for our sins (John 3:16–17).

The Gospel accounts dwell at length upon Jesus' death. Here is no mere appendix to a great life. It is the centerpiece of the entire action. According to the apostle Paul, "God demonstrates his own love for us in this: While we were still sinners, Christ died for us" (Romans 5:8).

What does it mean that Christ should have died for us? When a friend asks, "Would you go to the store for me?" she hopes you will go shopping instead of her, in her place. If you do not go, she will have to.

It is in this sense that Christ died for us: He died in our place. During those terrible hours on the cross, spiritual desolation engulfed Him. He was accepting the guilt of the world's sins—your sins, my sins, sins that cause separation between ourselves and God.

In a mysterious way beyond the limits of our understanding, the Father and the Son were separated while Jesus hung on the cross. At one point Jesus called out a verse from an Old Testament psalm that perfectly summarized what He was experiencing: "My God, my God, why have you forsaken me?" (Mark 15:34).

God Himself, in the person of His beloved Son, was accepting the guilt of humankind. Because Jesus died in our place, we can go free, free into life and beyond death into eternity. Our sins will no longer confront us in the final judgment. Because Jesus was temporarily separated from His Father for us (see 1 Peter 3:18–20), we can be reconciled with God through Him. This is what we mean when we call Jesus "Savior": He saves us from the consequences of our own wrongdoing.

This wonderful reconciliation between God and humanity can be ours, but it is not automatic. God has done His part, fully and perfectly. Nothing more remains to be done. He offers to forgive us, to clear our record (Psalm 103:10–12). But the question must be asked: Do we want to be forgiven?

No one is obliged to accept God's gift of forgiveness. The cross does not coerce us; it appeals to us.

"We implore you on Christ's behalf: Be reconciled to God. God made him who had no sin to be sin for us, so that in him we might become the righteousness of God" (2 Corinthians 5:20–21).

Millions of people have responded to God's love in Jesus Christ. I did myself, years ago, as I listened to a Christian speaker explaining what had happened at the cross. I knew the story, and yet that day it was as though I had never heard it before. I made my great decision before the day was out.

HE IS ALIVE!

Ancient epitaphs repeatedly betray a despairing outlook on death and the beyond.

"Child, be not overly distressed. I was not, I was born, I lived, I am not. . .that is all."

"All we are kept for death, fed like a herd of swine that are butchered, without rhyme or reason."

"Here lie I, Dionysius of Tarsus, sixty years old, unwed; would that my father had been the same."

By contrast the words of the New Testament shine with faith and confidence. Its message invaded the tired thinking of the Greek world, challenged the decadent philosophy of the Roman Empire—and finally superseded both. Gone were the shadowy hopes of the gray survival life beyond the grave. Gone were despair-bred attempts at postponing the end.

Here was a group of people transformed

by their buoyant conviction, based on the evidence of firsthand witnesses: Jesus had been raised from the grave. He was alive!

> *The Christian faith has been the greatest continuing germinator of human energy at all levels of which there is any record in the annals and achievements of man.*
>
> ARTHUR BRYANT, historian

Only such a rising can account for the empty tomb—and Romans, Jews, and disciples agreed that it was empty. Only a rising from the dead can explain the consistency of the reports and the astounding change that swept over the previously demoralized and scattered followers of Jesus.

And it is the risen Jesus, once crucified and now master of the world, who calls us, just as He called Peter, James, and John by the Galilean lake: "Follow me" (Matthew 4:19).

Without Jesus' resurrection, how could the greatest world movement ever known have possibly gotten of the ground at all?

Resurrection: Fact or Fiction?

Did Jesus of Nazareth really rise from the dead? Various alternative scenarios have been put forward.

The body of Jesus was stolen. Yet how could it have been, when an armed guard was posted to prevent that very thing? And why was the body never produced by Christ's enemies?

The whole thing was a result of wishful thinking. Apparently not, however, because the last thing the disciples seemed to be expecting was the resurrection of their leader. In any case, the authorities had only to go to the tomb to explode the fallacy immediately.

The stories of the resurrection were made up. But if the disciples were aware of some element of fraud, would they have risked their freedom and very lives to tell the world about the resurrection? Only an event of colossal magnitude would have given them the courage to face scorn, flogging, imprisonment, exile, and finally martyrdom.

BEGINNING WITH CHRIST

Following Jesus means developing a relationship, not mastering a technique.

For some, deciding to follow Him is like coming to a major crossroads. For others, it is like writing over in ink what was written in pencil many years before.

Baptism is associated with a new relationship with Jesus. The water symbolizes washing away the past and starting afresh.

It is an outward mark of the wonderful thing that has happened in their lives. And what is this wonderful thing? It is receiving the Spirit of Jesus Christ Himself by coming to Him, accepting forgiveness and God's love, and resolving—with God's help—to turn away from the old life and welcome in the new (2 Corinthians 5:17).

I have often explained this process as the Four R's.

Repent. I acknowledge in prayer that I have been a rebel before God. I may be a respectable member of society, but I have still been keeping Jesus at arm's length and living my life without any reference to Him. With Jesus' help, I do a U-turn. I declare that I have been wrong, that I am sorry, and that I am ready to battle against the self-centered habits of a lifetime.

Recognize. Who is it that I am receiving into my life? None other than Jesus Christ, the unique Son of God, the only true Savior of the world. I thank Him that He has died for the sins of the world and indeed for my sins. I recognize that Christ has done for me what I could never do for myself. Through His death upon the cross He has won forgiveness and eternal life for me, and He offers it as a gift. He has done it all.

Reflect. It costs nothing to become a Christian. But what are the implications of being a Christian? For instance, am I willing to declare war on all that I know is wrong in my life? Even if I don't feel strong enough to do this at present, am I willing to cooperate with God's Spirit as He reshapes my priorities and standards? Will I look to Jesus Christ for direction, to place my life under His rule? And am I willing to be known as one of Christ's followers? (A good way to begin is to confide in someone about the great decision you have made, perhaps by telling a church leader or by writing a letter to a friend.)

Receive. Here is a Bible promise: "To all who received him, to those who believed in his name, he gave the right to become children of God" (John 1:12). Now that Jesus is no longer here on earth but is in heaven, whom precisely are we receiving? It is the unseen Spirit of Jesus, the Holy Spirit, who comes to live within the believer.

But, you may wonder, how can I know that Christ has come to me?

There will be telltale signs. You begin to want to be with other believers. You find temptation becoming a real issue. The Bible's message means more to you than it did before.

Feelings fluctuate from person to person.

Some feel greatly relieved and joyful; others feel very little emotionally. That is really beside the point. The important thing is to take Jesus at His word and believe that He keeps His promises.

The promise that helped me to receive Christ years ago is contained in two sentences addressed by the risen Christ to a lukewarm church of nominal believers. Since I belonged to that category, it seemed particularly right for me. Here are His words: "Here I am! I stand at the door and knock. If anyone hears my voice and opens the door, I will come in and eat with him, and he with me" (Revelation 3:20).

So how do I open the door? In a prayer addressed to Jesus Christ. There is no neat formula. But in case it helps, opposite is a prayer inviting Christ to come in.

A PRAYER

Lord Jesus Christ,
*   I am aware that You are*
knocking upon the door of my
life, and I am grateful, for in my spirit
I am dead. I thank You for all the
things that have brought me to this
point in my life.

I am sorry that, knowingly and
unknowingly, I have rebelled and have
kept You at a distance.

With Your encouragement and
help, I now turn in repentance from
my old life that has had so much of
myself at the center.

With all my heart I thank You for
taking the guilt of my sins upon
Yourself at the cross.

I have reflected upon the implica-
tions of following You, and I declare
myself willing to fight against sin, to
be known as a Christian, and to follow
Your leadership.

I now receive You by faith, and I invite Your Spirit to enter my life and personality and to give me Your new, eternal life.

Come in, Lord Jesus, and with Your help, I will follow You, learn from You, and love You for the rest of my days. Amen.

FINAL EXAMINATION

From time to time I have a nightmare. I am back at college, about to take my final examinations all over again. It appears that I have done very little studying. Instead, I have been playing tennis, going out with my friends, and enjoying myself out on the river. Now I am caught unprepared.

In my dream I keep thinking to myself, *Why am I here? I thought I was a middle-aged pastor!* But the dream goes on, and the pressure mounts as the exam gets even closer. Finally I wake up. I lie in the darkness with waves of relief flooding over me. It's all right. It all happened years ago. And I passed.

Change the scene: It's your nightmare now. You are caught unprepared, and terror grips you. You walk into the classroom and pick up the examination. Calamity! Not a single question can you begin to answer. Your stomach turns over with fright, and your legs shake.

Just then a diminutive individual with

spectacles comes up behind you and taps you on the shoulder.

"Excuse me, you shouldn't be here."

"Shouldn't be here?" You feel dizzy.

"No, definitely not. You've already passed this examination."

"Passed?" The room sways.

"Oh yes. Our records show that you've passed. Look!" He waves a sheet of paper in front of your face. "Your diploma," explains the official. "So we don't want you here. You can go."

Dazedly, blindly, you stumble out of the classroom into the brilliant sunshine of a wonderful afternoon, the truth slowly sinking in. You have passed.

What is Christianity's good news? It is the amazing pronouncement to believers, here and now, that they have already passed from death to life. They are accepted, already forgiven, the present possessors of eternal life. Thanks to Jesus, God's judgment declares them "not guilty."

"I tell you the truth, whoever hears my

word and believes him who sent me has eternal life and will not be condemned; he has crossed over from death to life" (John 5:24).

We do not have to wait until we die to find out how we stand before God. We can know now.

THE FIGHT

It isn't going to be easy—not when I am following in the steps of a man who went to the cross. A day or two after my great decision to follow Jesus, I became aware of new forces tugging at me, even of a new bundle of problems that were not present before.

To be sure, the great problems of my relationship to God and my purpose and destination for life have been solved—but I begin to feel new tensions.

Not everybody is glad, it seems, that I have begun with God in a new way. I am frequently tempted to give in to old habits and attitudes.

I find it hard being a Christian at all.

If that is the case, then it is a very healthy sign. It would be bad for me if everything were easy. With no tensions, no struggles, I would never grow.

But in spite of my new crop of problems I press on, finding encouragement in the company of others who believe in Christ. After all, if Christianity is true, nothing else matters in the end.

> *I am not what I ought to be; I am not what I wish to be; I am not what I hope to be: but by the grace of God I am not what I was.*

JOHN NEWTON

John Newton was a godless slave trader who committed his life to God. He became a great hymn writer.

Why does someone become a Christian? Because of the wonderful friends that can be made in the Christian church? That is not the best reason. Because of the sense of peace and purpose that Christians often experience? That is not the best reason either.

The one valid reason for becoming a Christian is that Christianity is true. I want to be a Christian for truth's sake, even if the path I tread may be uncomfortable at times.

At least I have begun. Conflict only confirms me in my initial resolve.

KNOWING GOD

When I studied history at school, I was impressed by an account of a meeting between two great kings, Henry VIII of England and Francis I of France. In 1520 they met in Picardy in order to cement an alliance and impress each other with their wealth and power. To this end they erected a brilliant temporary palace. Everything in it was of the best quality, and all was spectacular. The "Field of the Cloth of Gold," they called it.

Their ultralavish display was soon dismantled, and less than thirty years later both kings were dead. By contrast our king, Jesus, will live forever. He is no less than the "King of kings" (1 Timothy 6:15), the "head of the church" (Ephesians 5:23), and the "firstborn over all creation" (Colossians 1:15)—as He is variously termed in the Bible. And He invites us to meet with Him.

You can have your own Field of the Cloth of Gold wherever you are. You can meet God privately in your room. Or you can gather a few believers in someone's house and together meet the master of all the universe.

Jesus has promised that whenever two or three meet together in His name, He will join them as the unseen presence (Matthew 18:20). He has also promised to hear us if we come to Him alone (Matthew 6:6). We do not need a massive palace or even a thick pile carpet. The glory is not in the royal trappings but in the fact that Christ has promised to be with us as our leader and companion "to the very end of the age" (Matthew 28:20).

As we awake in the morning and the film of the day ahead begins to roll before our minds, we can commit the day to Christ, bringing our concerns and our friends to God.

DISCOVERING PRAYER

Prayer opens a whole world to our Christian influence. Some Christians use a prayer diary, or prayer list, containing the names of those people for whom God's blessing and help is desired.

Prayer builds up a relationship with the Lord. It is nothing like putting a coin in a vending machine. It is not a way of persuading God to do our bidding. It is the way He wants us to cooperate with Him in fulfilling His purposes for this world.

Prayer helps us. Nothing else is quite so valuable to the life of the believer as this wonderful approach to our king. And in the end our quiet times in His presence will be more effective—and far more lasting—than any Field of the Cloth of Gold.

THE HOLY SPIRIT

It takes a while, but believers in Jesus Christ steadily learn that we are put in this world not to be consumers primarily, but contributors.

We are called to become like Jesus Christ in character. And we are called to serve Him in a world of great needs and opportunities, directing others to His love by the example of our lives and our words of testimony.

I read in a book that a man called Christ went about doing good. It is very disconcerting that I am so easily satisfied with just going about.

KAGAWA OF JAPAN

We sense that this is beyond us. It would be, but for the presence of His Spirit in our lives. The Holy Spirit comes into the life of a believer from day one, so a Christian can begin to serve God immediately. True, we may know very little, but we can still be servants.

As our knowledge of the Bible increases, and as we learn to place our lives every day at God's disposal, the Holy Spirit uses us in a wide variety of ways to build and encourage the church members around us and to introduce an unbelieving world to Christ's claims.

But how can we allow the Spirit to work most effectively in us?

We must clear the blockages in our lives. We must confess the sins that would otherwise spoil and compromise our Christian witness.

We should make Jesus the Lord of every day. We should do our best to obey His desires and live out the message of the Bible.

We should share our Christian blessings with others. Paradoxically, the way to be filled is to be emptied! We may not believe that at first. But as we begin to expend our energies in serving others, we find that we feel better and more fulfilled.

THE LAST WORD

God, heavenly Father,
The story of my life is like the writing of a book. The dawning of each day is like turning a fresh new page, white and clean, perfectly blank, waiting to be filled with actions and words.

I am ashamed when I think of those earlier pages, of the volume of days that went to make up the story of my life.

It was Your Son who made the difference to my record, by His entry into our world.

Living and dying, He wrote a new story, my story.

Father, let me dedicate this new day to You, in love and gratitude for all that You have done.

May today bring the writing of a new fresh page, the story of my life in Yours and Yours in mine. Amen.

Inspirational Library

Beautiful purse/pocket-size editions of Christian classics bound in flexible leatherette. These books make thoughtful gifts for everyone on your list, including yourself!

When I'm on My Knees　　　The highly popular collection of devotional thoughts on prayer, especially for women.
　　　Flexible Leatherette $4.97

The Bible Promise Book　　　Over 1,000 promises from God's Word arranged by topic. What does God promise about matters like: Anger, Illness, Jealousy, Love, Money, Old Age, and Mercy? Find out in this book!
　　　Flexible Leatherette $3.97

Daily Wisdom for Women　　　A daily devotional for women seeking biblical wisdom to apply to their lives. Scripture taken from the New American Standard Version of the Bible.
　　　Flexible Leatherette $4.97

My Daily Prayer Journal　　　Each page is dated and features a Scripture verse and ample room for you to record your thoughts, prayers, and praises. One page for each day of the year.
　　　Flexible Leatherette $4.97

Available wherever books are sold.
Or order from:

Barbour Publishing, Inc.
P.O. Box 719
Uhrichsville, OH 44683
http://www.barbourbooks.com

If you order by mail, add $2.00 to your order for shipping.
Prices are subject to change without notice.